EMPOWERED HOMEMAKERS: BREAKING BOUNDARIES

The Strength Within: Empowering Women

Raghavi Uppuluri

ISBN 9798894984643

Dedication

To my Mother, Mother-in-law, daughter, and all the powerful women who have proven that marriage is not a barrier to pursuing their dreams. Your courage, resilience, and determination have paved the way for countless others to believe in themselves and strive for greatness.

To all the women around me who aspire to success in life, may this book serve as a beacon of inspiration and empowerment. May you find the strength to pursue your dreams, defy expectations, and achieve fulfillment in every aspect of your journey.

Your unwavering support and belief in me have fueled my own aspirations. This book is dedicated to each of you with heartfelt gratitude and admiration for the incredible women you are.

This dedication recognizes the influential women in your life and acknowledges their impact on your journey and those of others striving for success and fulfillment.

CONTENTS

PREFACE

The decision to embark on this writing journey was born from a deep-seated observation of a phenomenon that resonates with many of us—particularly women who have chosen to prioritize family responsibilities over their professional aspirations. In my circle of friends and acquaintances, I have witnessed the quiet, sometimes unspoken regret that lingers among those who feel they have sacrificed their career ambitions for the sake of familial duties. This sentiment is not unique to a few individuals but rather a pervasive feeling that touches many lives.

I have seen friends who, after getting married and starting families, put their careers on hold or made compromises that led them away from their original dreams. They often speak of the paths not taken, the opportunities missed, and the sense of unfulfilled potential. This experience, shared by so many, sparked a deep desire within me to explore and illuminate a path forward—a path that reconciles the responsibilities of family life with the pursuit of personal and professional fulfillment.

INTRODUCTION: THE POWER OF CHOICE

The power of choice is a fundamental right for every individual, including housewives. While family and household responsibilities may sometimes seem like barriers to pursuing personal aspirations, it's essential to remember that there are always opportunities within reach, even within the constraints of time and responsibilities.

Housewives can empower themselves by recognizing their own agency and actively seeking out ways to balance their personal aspirations with their family duties. This might involve exploring part-time job opportunities, starting a home-based business, or pursuing flexible work arrangements that accommodate their schedules.

It's crucial for housewives to understand that their dreams and aspirations are valid, and they deserve the opportunity to pursue them. By carefully planning and prioritizing their goals, they can create pathways to professional fulfillment while fulfilling their responsibilities at home.

Ultimately, it's all about embracing the power of choice and making decisions that align with one's passions, values, and life circumstances. Whether it's pursuing a career, starting a business, or finding fulfillment through other avenues, every housewife deserves the freedom to shape her own path and pursue her dreams.

In today's world, women are increasingly empowered to make choices that shape their professional lives. This empowerment extends beyond mere decisions about where and how to work; it encompasses the freedom to define success on their own terms and to balance career aspirations with personal fulfillment. This essay explores the significance of choice in women's careers, focusing on how it influences their paths from home-based work to office environments. By examining the benefits and challenges associated with these choices, we gain insight into the broader implications for gender equality and individual empowerment.

1. The Evolution of Women's Roles in the Workplace

Historically, women's participation in the workforce has evolved significantly. From being predominantly homemakers to seeking equal opportunities in various professions, women have progressively asserted their capabilities and contributions. The shift toward gender equality has paved the way for women to explore diverse career paths and to challenge traditional stereotypes about their roles in society.

It's true that women have always had the capability to excel in multiple roles and manage them effectively. Throughout history, women have demonstrated their abilities in various fields, such as leadership, academia, business, and many others.

In recent times, there has been a growing recognition of the importance of gender equality, which aims to ensure that women have equal opportunities to participate and succeed in all aspects of life, including education, career advancement, and decision-making roles. When given the chance, women have proven themselves capable of not only performing at par with men but often bringing unique perspectives and skills to the table.

However, achieving true gender equality is an ongoing process that involves addressing systemic barriers, stereotypes, and biases that may hinder women's progress. It's important to continue working toward creating environments where women and men can contribute equally based on their abilities and talents rather than being limited by societal expectations or prejudices.

2. The Rise of Flexible Work Arrangements

One of the pivotal changes in recent years has been the rise of flexible work arrangements. This includes options such as remote work, part-time schedules, and job sharing, which provide women with greater flexibility to manage their professional responsibilities alongside personal commitments. Remote work, in particular has gained popularity due to advancements in technology, allowing women to work from home or any location with internet access.

Advancements like remote work and flexible work arrangements have significantly benefited women in balancing their personal and professional lives. These options allow women to manage their time more effectively, juggling responsibilities both at home and in their careers.

Having the ability to work from home or to have flexible hours can be particularly advantageous for women who might otherwise face challenges balancing traditional household responsibilities with their professional aspirations. It enables them to pursue their career goals without having to sacrifice their personal priorities.

Moreover, these flexible opportunities empower women to make bold decisions about their careers. They can choose to pursue professional paths, explore new opportunities, and achieve their aspirations while still fulfilling their responsibilities at home.

However, it's important to note that while flexible work options can be a significant step forward, there are still barriers and challenges that women may face in the workplace, such as gender bias, unequal pay, and lack of representation in leadership roles. Continued efforts toward creating inclusive work environments and addressing these issues are essential to ensure that all individuals, regardless of gender, have equal opportunities to thrive in their careers.

3. Benefits of Working from Home

Working from home offers numerous benefits for women. It provides flexibility in managing work hours, allowing them to juggle career demands with family responsibilities more effectively. Remote work also reduces commuting time and costs, promotes a better work-life balance, and may contribute to increased job satisfaction and productivity.

Absolutely, working from home offers significant benefits, especially for women who may need flexibility due to personal responsibilities. Here are some advantages of remote work that cater to managing professional work alongside personal commitments:

⇨ Flexibility in Hours: Remote work allows women to schedule their work hours around personal responsibilities such as childcare, eldercare, or other household duties. This flexibility enables them to find a balance that works for them.

⇨ Commuting Stress: Working from home eliminates commuting time and costs, providing more time for both work and personal activities. This can reduce stress and contribute to a better work-life balance.

⇨ Improved Productivity: Many find they are more productive when working remotely due to fewer interruptions and the ability to create a personalized work environment.

⇨ Cost Savings: Remote work often results in savings on transportation, work attire, and eating out, which can be beneficial for managing household finances.

⇨ Career Advancement Opportunities: Remote work options can enable women to continue advancing in their careers while managing personal responsibilities. They can remain professionally engaged and relevant without being constrained by traditional office hours.

⇨ Health Benefits: Remote work can contribute to better health outcomes by reducing exposure to workplace stressors, promoting a healthier work-life balance, and allowing more time for self-care activities.

⇨ Inclusive Work Environment: Remote work options can foster a more inclusive workplace, accommodating diverse needs and promoting a culture of trust and empowerment.

⇨ Skill Development: Working remotely often requires developing skills in time management, communication, and technology use, which can enhance overall professional growth.

⇨ Global Opportunities: Remote work can open up opportunities to work with teams and clients from around the world, expanding professional networks and perspectives.

⇨ Environmental Impact: Reduced commuting and office space usage can contribute to a smaller carbon footprint, supporting sustainability efforts.

In summary, the option to work from home provides women with the flexibility and autonomy to structure their careers around their personal responsibilities, thereby promoting work-life balance and overall well-being.

4. Challenges of Working from Home

Absolutely, while working from home offers flexibility, it also presents unique challenges for women, especially when managing work alongside childcare or other household responsibilities. Here are some common challenges women may face when working from home:

⇨ Managing Household Responsibilities: Balancing work tasks with household chores, childcare, and family responsibilities can be overwhelming. Women often find themselves multi-tasking to meet both professional and personal demands.

⇨ Distractions and Interruptions: The home environment can be less structured than an office, leading to more distractions from family members, pets, household tasks, and personal errands.

⇨ Lack of Dedicated Workspace: Not having a dedicated office space can impact concentration and productivity. Women may struggle to create a suitable work environment amidst household clutter or noise.

⇨ Isolation and Lack of Social Interaction: Remote work can be isolating, lacking the social interactions and support network found in a traditional office setting. This can affect morale and mental well-being.

⇨ Technology and Connectivity Issues: Dealing with technical issues, unreliable internet connections, or inadequate equipment can disrupt work tasks, especially during virtual meetings or calls.

⇨ Boundary Setting: Establishing clear boundaries between work and personal life can be challenging when working from home. It may be difficult to disconnect from work outside of designated hours.

⇨ Career Progression and Visibility: Remote work may impact visibility within the organization and opportunities for career advancement, especially if face-to-face interactions and networking are limited.

⇨ Work-Life Balance: While remote work offers flexibility, it can blur the boundaries between work and personal life, making it difficult to switch off from work-related stressors.

⇨ Stress and Burnout: Juggling multiple responsibilities and feeling pressured to excel in both professional and personal roles can lead to stress and burnout over time.

Despite these challenges, many women successfully navigate remote work by leveraging support systems, adopting time management strategies, and prioritizing self-care. Organizations can also support women by offering flexible policies, resources for remote work, and acknowledging the unique challenges they may face. With determination and resilience, women can overcome these obstacles and thrive in their careers while balancing personal responsibilities.

5. Advantages of Office-based Work Environments

Absolutely, women starting their careers at mid-age can face specific challenges in a traditional office-based environment, but they also have unique opportunities for growth and development. Here are some points highlighting both the challenges and advantages:

Challenges:

⇨ Balancing Responsibilities: Managing both professional responsibilities and personal commitments can be demanding, especially if they have caregiving responsibilities or other family obligations.

⇨ Adjusting to Workplace Culture: Adapting to the workplace culture and dynamics may take time, particularly if they are transitioning from a different career path or returning to work after a break

⇨ Technological Adaptation: Depending on their previous work experience, mid-career starters may need to familiarize themselves with new technologies and tools used in the office environment.

⇨ Career Progression: Starting a career later in life may pose challenges in terms of catching up with peers in terms of seniority or career progression.

Advantages:

⇨ Face-to-Face Interactions: Working in an office allows for direct face-to-face interactions with colleagues, clients, and managers. This can enhance communication skills, build professional relationships, and boost confidence.

⇨ Career Progression: Starting a career later in life may pose challenges in terms of catching up with peers in terms of seniority or career progression.

⇨ Learning Opportunities: Being in a physical office environment provides opportunities for on-the-job learning, mentorship, and professional development that may not be as readily available in remote settings

⇨ Networking: Office-based work facilitates networking and collaboration with a diverse group of professionals, which can open doors to new opportunities and career advancement.

⇨ Social Support and Motivation: Interacting with colleagues in person can provide emotional support, motivation, and inspiration from observing others who have successfully navigated similar career paths.

⇨ Structured Environment: An office environment offers a structured routine and dedicated workspace, which can enhance productivity and focus compared to remote work setups.

⇨ Professional Visibility: Being physically present in the office can increase visibility within the organization, potentially leading to greater recognition for achievements and career growth opportunities.

Strategies for Success:

⇨ Time Management: Prioritize tasks, set clear boundaries between work and personal life, and leverage time management techniques to balance responsibilities effectively

⇨ Seek Mentorship: Connect with mentors or peers who can provide guidance and support in navigating the workplace and advancing your career goals.

⇨ Continuous Learning: Stay updated with industry trends and seek out opportunities for professional development to enhance skills and knowledge.

⇨ Build Relationships: Actively engage with colleagues and build a professional network within and outside the organization to foster career growth and opportunities.

⇨ Self-Care: Prioritize self-care to maintain well-being and manage stress effectively, ensuring sustainable career success.

In conclusion, while starting a career at mid-age in an office-based environment may present challenges, it also offers valuable opportunities for personal and professional growth through face-to-face interactions, networking, and learning experiences. With determination, resilience, and proactive strategies, women can successfully navigate these challenges and thrive in their careers.

6. Balancing Career Aspirations and Personal Priorities

Absolutely, planning and balancing career aspirations with personal priorities are essential steps for women aiming to achieve their goals. Here are some key points to consider when creating a plan

⇨ Set Clear Goals: Define your career aspirations and personal priorities clearly. This clarity helps in understanding what you want to achieve professionally and what matters most in your personal life.

⇨ Assess Current Commitments: Evaluate your current commitments, including family responsibilities, hobbies, health, and other personal obligations. Understanding these will help in creating a realistic plan.

⇨ Prioritize Tasks: Prioritize tasks and activities based on their importance and urgency. This will help you allocate time and resources effectively between your career and personal life.

⇨ Time Management: Develop strong time management skills to optimize your daily schedule. This includes setting aside dedicated time for work, personal activities, relaxation, and self-care.

⇨ Seek Support: Build a support network of family members, friends, mentors, and colleagues who can provide assistance and encouragement as you pursue your goals.

⇨ Flexibility and Adaptability: Recognize that plans may need adjustment as circumstances change. Remain flexible and adapt your strategies as needed to maintain balance.

⇨ Self-Care: Prioritize self-care to maintain physical, mental, and emotional well-being. This includes adequate rest, nutrition, exercise, and time for relaxation.

⇨ Continuous Learning: Stay curious and continuously seek opportunities for learning and growth in both your personal and professional life.

⇨ Celebrate Milestones: Acknowledge and celebrate your achievements, no matter how small. This boosts motivation and reinforces your commitment to your goals.

⇨ Reflect and Adjust: Regularly review your plan, reflect on your progress, and make adjustments as necessary. This iterative process ensures you stay aligned with your aspirations and priorities.

By creating a thoughtful plan that integrates both career aspirations and personal priorities, women can effectively manage the balance and achieve fulfillment in both areas of their lives. With determination, resilience, and support, they can overcome challenges and realize their full potential.

Conclusion

Giving women the power to choose their career paths is a big step toward making sure everyone is treated fairly and equally. When workplaces offer flexible ways of working and appreciate the different things women can do, it helps them do well and make a real difference in their jobs and communities.

As we keep pushing for everyone to have the same chances and help women reach their career goals, let's celebrate how strong and determined they are. Embracing different ways of working and letting women decide what's best for them makes workplaces better for everyone.

In short, the power of choice for women isn't just about deciding where to work. It's about having the freedom to pick careers that match what they want to do and making society more fair and open for everyone.

02

BREAKING STEREOTYPES: CHALLENGING TRADITIONAL ROLES

Housewives can challenge themselves to pursue careers that interest them. They have incredible inner strength, fulfilling roles as wives, mothers, daughters-in-law, sisters, and daughters, giving their best in each role. Why not challenge themselves to take on a professional career as employees, too? By embracing challenges, they can achieve anything they set their minds to. Women are naturally capable of juggling multiple responsibilities, and by taking on professional roles, they can break stereotypes and reach their goals.

Housewives possess immense potential and strength as they navigate various roles in their families and communities. They excel as caregivers, organizers, and problem-solvers, often managing complex

household responsibilities with efficiency and dedication. These roles require a diverse skill set, including time management, interpersonal skills, budgeting, and decision-making—all of which are valuable in a professional setting.

For example, a housewife who manages the household finances effectively demonstrates financial management skills that could translate well into a career in accounting or financial planning. Similarly, organizing family schedules and activities showcases strong organizational and planning abilities that are crucial in project management or event coordination roles.

Challenging themselves to pursue a professional career allows housewives to harness their existing skills and develop new ones. They can seek opportunities to return to education or training, explore internships or volunteer work to gain practical experience, or even start small businesses based on their interests and talents.

Moreover, women inherently possess the resilience and adaptability needed to excel in various roles simultaneously. By choosing to enter the workforce, they not only contribute financially to their families but also expand their personal growth and fulfillment. This decision challenges traditional stereotypes about women's roles and demonstrates their capability to thrive in diverse professional environments.

For instance, many successful women have transitioned from being full-time caregivers to establishing careers in fields such as entrepreneurship, education, healthcare, technology, and more. They have shown that with determination and support, they can break barriers and achieve their career aspirations.

Here are more examples that illustrate how women can break stereotypes by pursuing careers traditionally considered outside their expected roles:

⇨ Engineering and Technology: Historically, male-dominated fields like engineering and technology have increasingly welcomed women. For example, a former homemaker with a passion for problem-solving and technology may pursue a career in software development or engineering, challenging the stereotype that women aren't suited for technical roles.

⇨ Construction and Trades: Women entering construction and trades, such as carpentry, plumbing, or electrician work, defy stereotypes about physical strength and suitability for these professions. They showcase that skill and determination matter more than gender.

⇨ Politics and Leadership: Women entering politics and leadership positions challenge stereotypes about gender roles in decision-making and governance. They demonstrate that leadership qualities like empathy, negotiation skills, and strategic thinking are not gender-specific.

⇨ Military and Defense: In many countries, women are increasingly joining military and defense forces, challenging stereotypes about combat roles and physical capabilities. They prove that dedication, discipline, and teamwork are essential qualities regardless of gender.

⇨ Entrepreneurship: Starting and leading successful businesses challenges stereotypes about women's roles as homemakers or support personnel. Female entrepreneurs across various industries showcase innovation, leadership, and business acumen.

⇨ Sports and Fitness: Women excelling in sports and fitness coaching or becoming professional athletes challenge stereotypes about physical prowess and leadership in sports traditionally dominated by men.

⇨ STEM Education and Advocacy: Women in STEM (Science, Technology, Engineering, and Mathematics) fields not only contribute to groundbreaking research and innovation but also advocate for gender equality and representation in these fields, challenging stereotypes about women's interests and abilities in science and technology.

⇨ Creative Arts and Entertainment: Women breaking into traditionally male-dominated areas of creative arts, such as directing, filmmaking, and music production, challenge stereotypes about creativity and leadership in the entertainment industry.

⇨ Legal and Judicial Roles: Women serving as judges, lawyers, and legal professionals challenge stereotypes about gender bias in law and justice. They advocate for fairness and equality under the law.

⇨ Agriculture and Farming: Women involved in agriculture and farming, including owning and managing farms or agricultural businesses, challenge stereotypes about manual labor and leadership in rural industries.

⇨ These examples highlight how women across different sectors and industries are challenging stereotypes and paving the way for future generations to pursue their aspirations without limitations based on gender.

Their achievements contribute to a more inclusive society where everyone's talents and contributions are valued equally.

Conclusion:

By embracing the challenge of pursuing a professional career, housewives not only empower themselves but also inspire others. They exemplify the limitless potential of women to excel in multiple roles and contribute meaningfully to both their families and society. This journey toward personal and professional fulfillment is a testament to their strength, resilience, and determination to defy expectations and reach their goals.

03

DISCOVERING YOUR PASSIONS AND SKILLS

Spending time alone to think about what you're good at and what you enjoy is important for figuring out what job you might like. When you know your skills, you understand what you're best at doing. This helps you pick a job that suits you well, so you're more likely to do well and feel happy in your work.

Being passionate about your job is also really important. When you love what you do, it feels fun and exciting, not like a boring task. Choosing a job that matches your passions lets you do meaningful work that makes you feel good and helps others.

When you combine knowing yourself with doing what you love, you can start a job that's not just about money but also makes you feel happy inside. It's all about picking a career that matches who you are and what makes you feel important.

⇨ **Skill Assessment**: Assess your existing skills and experiences gained from managing household responsibilities. Skills like organization, time management, budgeting, and multitasking are valuable in many professions.

⇨ Exploring Options: Research different career paths and industries that interest you. Consider flexible or remote work options that accommodate your family responsibilities.

⇨ Education and Training: Pursue additional education or training if needed to acquire new skills or certifications relevant to your chosen career path.

⇨ Networking: Build a professional network by connecting with others in your desired industry. Attend networking events, join online communities, and seek mentorship opportunities.

⇨ Support System: Seek support from family, friends, and community resources to help balance your career aspirations with household responsibilities. Communicate openly with your family about your career goals.

⇨ Time Management: Develop effective time management strategies to juggle work commitments and family responsibilities. Prioritize tasks and set realistic goals to maintain a healthy work-life balance.

⇨ Self-Care: Prioritize self-care to maintain physical, mental, and emotional well-being while pursuing career ambitions. Take breaks, exercise, and engage in activities that help you recharge.

⇨ Financial Planning: Consider the financial implications of starting a career, including potential costs for education, training, or childcare. Create a budget and plan accordingly to manage expenses.

⇨ Continuous Learning: Stay updated with industry trends and developments by engaging in lifelong learning. Attend workshops, webinars, or online courses to expand your knowledge and skills.

⇨ Resilience and Persistence: Stay resilient and persistent in pursuing your career goals. Recognize that challenges may arise, but your determination and perseverance will help you overcome obstacles.

Conclusion:

These points aim to empower housewives who are considering starting a career by providing practical advice and encouragement to pursue their aspirations while managing their household responsibilities effectively.

04

EXPLORING CAREER OPTIONS: FROM HOME TO WORKPLACE

Absolutely! In today's digitally-driven world, there is a vast array of career opportunities available for individuals to explore and grow. The rise of digitalization has democratized access to employment, allowing people from diverse backgrounds and qualifications to find opportunities for meaningful work.

Public platforms such as YouTube, Instagram, Twitter, and Facebook have revolutionized the way individuals can showcase their creativity and skills, opening doors to self-employment and entrepreneurship. Whether it's creating content, offering services, or selling products, these platforms provide a level playing field for anyone with a passion and a vision to pursue their career aspirations.

One of the remarkable aspects of these opportunities is the flexibility they offer. With the ability to work from home and set their own schedules, individuals have the autonomy to balance their professional pursuits with their personal lives. This flexibility enables them to work on their terms, in environments that suit their comfort and preferences.

Moreover, the digital landscape is continuously evolving, creating new avenues for innovation and growth. From freelancing and remote work to e-commerce and digital marketing, there are countless paths to explore and opportunities to seize. With creativity, determination, and adaptability, individuals can carve out successful careers in this dynamic and ever-expanding digital ecosystem.

Ultimately, the democratization of career opportunities through digital platforms empowers individuals to take control of their professional destinies, pursue their passions, and unlock their full potential. By harnessing the power of digitalization, anyone can embark on a journey of self-employment, creativity, and fulfillment in today's interconnected world.

⇨ Skills Audit: Conduct a thorough audit of your skills, including both technical and soft skills. Identify areas where you excel and areas where you may need further development.

⇨ Industry Insights: Gain insights into different industries by attending industry-specific events, conferences, or workshops. This can help you understand industry norms, challenges, and opportunities.

⇨ Job Shadowing: Consider shadowing professionals in your desired field to get a firsthand experience of their day-to-day responsibilities and to assess if it aligns with your interests.

⇨ Professional Development: Invest in professional development opportunities such as certifications, workshops, or online courses that can enhance your skills and marketability.

⇨ Side Projects: Undertake side projects or freelance work related to your desired career path to build experience and a portfolio of work that showcases your abilities.

⇨ Informational Interviews: Conduct informational interviews with professionals working in your target industry. Ask about their career paths, challenges they faced, and advice they have for newcomers.

⇨ Job Fit Assessment: Utilize online assessments or tools to determine how well your skills and personality traits match with different job roles and work environments.

⇨ Explore Non-traditional Careers: Consider emerging or non-traditional career paths that may align with your interests and skills, such as digital nomadism, virtual assistance, or content creation.

⇨ Cultural Fit: Assess the organizational culture of potential employers to ensure it aligns with your values, work style, and expectations for work-life balance.

⇨ Personal Branding: Develop a strong personal brand online through LinkedIn, professional portfolios, and social media platforms. This can enhance your visibility and credibility within your chosen field.

These points provide a broader perspective on exploring career options by focusing on skills assessment, industry immersion, professional growth, and aligning personal values with career aspirations. They aim to facilitate a well-rounded approach to finding a career that not only matches your skills but also fulfills your professional and personal goals.

05

OVERCOMING SELF-DOUBT AND FEAR

Self-doubt and fear are common experiences for everyone, but they should not hold us back from pursuing our dreams and aspirations. Overcoming these barriers requires practice, perseverance, and a clear understanding of our goals and desires.

Whether it's choosing to be a housewife or striving for financial independence, clarity about our aspirations is essential for motivation and progress. Once we have a clear vision of what we want to achieve, we can begin to identify the barriers that stand in our way and work toward overcoming them.

One effective strategy is to focus on building our skills and capabilities. By continuously learning and improving ourselves, we gain confidence and competence in our chosen pursuits. This not only helps us overcome self-doubt but also equips us with the tools and knowledge needed to navigate challenges and achieve success.

Moreover, it's important to confront our fears head-on and take proactive steps to address them. Whether it's fear of failure, fear of judgment, or fear of the unknown, facing our fears allows us to reclaim our power and move forward with courage and determination.

By embracing a growth mindset and viewing challenges as opportunities for growth and learning, we can overcome self-doubt and fear and realize our full potential. With persistence, resilience, and a commitment to self-improvement, we can break free from limitations and create the life we desire.

Self-doubt and fear can present significant disadvantages for women, impacting various aspects of their lives:

⇨ Undermined Confidence: Self-doubt can erode confidence levels, making it harder for women to assert themselves in personal relationships, professional settings, or when pursuing their goals.

⇨ Limited Opportunities: Fear of failure or rejection can lead women to avoid taking risks or pursuing new opportunities, potentially limiting their career advancement or personal growth.

⇨ Impact on Mental Health: Persistent self-doubt and fear can contribute to anxiety, stress, and even depression, affecting overall well-being and quality of life.

⇨ Holding Back from Speaking Up: In group settings or decision-making scenarios, self-doubt may prevent women from expressing their ideas or opinions, leading to missed opportunities to contribute meaningfully.

⇨ Difficulty in Setting and Achieving Goals: Fear can paralyze initiative, making it challenging for women to set ambitious goals and take the necessary steps to achieve them.

⇨ Impostor Syndrome: Many women experience impostor syndrome, feeling like they don't deserve their accomplishments or are not as competent as others perceive them to be, which can undermine career progression and personal satisfaction.

⇨ Impact on Relationships: Self-doubt and fear can affect personal relationships, leading to difficulties in communication, trust issues, and missed opportunities for emotional connection.

Addressing self-doubt and overcoming fears often involves building self-awareness, developing resilience, seeking support from mentors or counselors, and gradually pushing beyond comfort zones. By doing so, women can unlock their full potential and pursue their aspirations with greater confidence and determination.

Overcoming self-doubt and fear is crucial for any woman looking to start a career. Here are some specific points to address these challenges:

⇨ Positive Self-Talk: Replace negative thoughts with positive affirmations. Remind yourself of your strengths, skills, and past achievements.

⇨ Set Realistic Goals: Break down your career goals into smaller, manageable steps. Celebrate each achievement along the way to boost your confidence.

⇨ Seek Support: Surround yourself with supportive people who believe in you. This could be friends, family members, or mentors who can provide encouragement and advice.

⇨ Professional Development: Invest in upgrading your skills and knowledge through courses, workshops, or certifications. This can increase your confidence in your abilities.

⇨ Network Strategically: Attend networking events, join professional associations, and connect with others in your desired field. Networking can open doors to opportunities and provide valuable insights.

⇨ Challenge Negative Beliefs: Identify and challenge limiting beliefs about your age or abilities. Focus on the value and experience you bring to the table.

⇨ Embrace Lifelong Learning: Recognize that learning is a continuous process. Stay curious and open to acquiring new skills and knowledge relevant to your career aspirations.

⇨ Take Calculated Risks: Step outside your comfort zone and take calculated risks. This could involve applying for challenging roles or starting a business venture aligned with your passions.

⇨ Practice Self-Care: Prioritize self-care to maintain your physical, mental, and emotional well-being. This includes adequate rest, exercise, and activities that rejuvenate you.

⇨ Visualize Success: Visualize yourself succeeding in your new career. Create a vision board or write down your goals to reinforce your commitment and belief in your abilities.

By focusing on these points, you can gradually build confidence, overcome self-doubt, and pursue a fulfilling career path at any stage of life. Remember, it's never too late to start something new and meaningful.

06

BUILDING CONFIDENCE AND RESILIENCE

Confidence and resilience are indeed essential ingredients for success in life, and they are qualities that can be developed and nurtured over time.

Confidence is not something we are necessarily born with; it is something that we cultivate through our experiences, challenges, and accomplishments. By setting goals, stepping out of our comfort zones, and embracing opportunities to learn and grow, we can gradually build our confidence and belief in ourselves.

Resilience, on the other hand, is the ability to bounce back from setbacks, adapt to change, and persevere in the face of adversity. Like water, which can flow and take the shape of its container, human beings have the capacity to adapt to different situations and circumstances. By cultivating resilience, we can weather life's storms with grace and emerge stronger and more resilient than before.

Just as water continues to flow and never stops, so too should we continue to learn, grow, and adapt to the challenges and opportunities that come our way. By embracing a mindset of resilience and adopting a flexible approach to life, we can navigate obstacles and setbacks with confidence and determination.

Ultimately, by building our confidence and resilience, we empower ourselves to overcome challenges, seize opportunities, and achieve success in both our personal and professional lives. Like water, we have the capacity to flow, adapt, and thrive in any environment.

Here are some more detailed strategies tailored to help women build confidence:

⇨ Identify Strengths: Make a list of your strengths, skills, and achievements. Recognizing what you excel at can boost your self-assurance.

⇨ Set Clear Goals: Define clear, achievable goals for yourself. Break them down into smaller steps and celebrate each milestone you reach.

⇨ Challenge Negative Thought: Notice when you have self-doubting thoughts and challenge them with more realistic and positive perspectives. For example, if you think, "I'm not good enough," remind yourself of times when you succeeded or received positive feedback.

⇨ Practice Self-Compassion: Treat yourself with kindness and understanding, especially when facing setbacks or failures. Understand that everyone makes mistakes, and it's an opportunity to learn and grow.

⇨ Develop Assertiveness: Practice expressing your thoughts, opinions, and needs assertively. Start with small situations and gradually build up to more challenging ones.

⇨ Seek Learning Opportunities: Continuously seek opportunities to learn and develop new skills. Knowledge and competence can significantly boost confidence.

⇨ Surround Yourself with Supportive People: Build a network of supportive friends, family members, mentors, or peers who encourage and believe in you.

⇨ Physical Well-being: Taking care of your physical health through regular exercise, proper nutrition, and sufficient rest can positively impact your confidence and overall well-being.

⇨ Face Your Fears: Identify specific fears or challenges that hold you back and take small steps to confront them. Each small success will increase your confidence to tackle bigger challenges.

⇨ Celebrate Progress: Acknowledge and celebrate your progress, no matter how small. Recognizing your efforts and achievements reinforces a positive self-image.

Building confidence is a gradual process that involves self-reflection, practice, and self-compassion. By implementing these strategies consistently, women can cultivate greater confidence to pursue their aspirations and navigate life's challenges with resilience.

Here are some additional points on building resilience specifically for women:

⇨ Embrace Vulnerability: Recognize that it's okay to feel vulnerable at times. Being open about your emotions and seeking support when needed strengthens resilience.

⇨ Develop Assertiveness Skills: Practice asserting your needs and boundaries in various aspects of life, which fosters self-confidence and resilience in challenging situations.

⇨ Cultivate Emotional Intelligence: Improve your ability to understand and manage your emotions effectively. This includes recognizing triggers, practicing empathy toward yourself and others, and developing resilience in emotional responses.

⇨ Foster Positive Self-Image: Focus on nurturing a positive self-image and self-worth. Challenge negative self-talk and replace it with affirmations that reinforce your strengths and capabilities.

⇨ Engage in Lifelong Learning: Continuously seek opportunities for personal and professional growth. Learning new skills and knowledge enhances adaptability and resilience in the face of change.

⇨ Practice Gratitude: Regularly reflect on things you are grateful for. Gratitude cultivates a positive outlook and resilience by shifting focus from challenges to blessings.

⇨ Strengthen Boundaries: Establish clear boundaries in relationships and commitments. Respecting your own limits helps prevent burnout and maintains emotional resilience.

⇨ Stay Connected to Your Values: Align your actions and decisions with your core values. This connection provides a sense of purpose and direction during difficult times.

⇨ Engage in Physical Activity: Regular exercise and physical activity not only promote physical health but also reduce stress and boost mental resilience.

⇨ Celebrate Resilience: Acknowledge and celebrate your resilience in overcoming past challenges. Reflect on how you have grown stronger as a result of adversity.

By incorporating these strategies into daily life, women can build and strengthen their resilience, enabling them to navigate life's uncertainties and challenges with greater confidence and effectiveness.

07

SKILLS FOR SUCCESS: ENHANCING YOUR PROFESSIONAL TOOLKIT

Once you identify your skills, it's crucial to focus on continuously improving and honing them to excel in your chosen profession. Here's a breakdown of steps to follow:

⇨ Identify Your Skills: Start by identifying your strengths and areas of expertise. Reflect on past experiences, feedback from others, and activities you enjoy doing. This will help you understand where your talents lie and what skills you possess.

⇨ Set Clear Goals: Define your career goals and aspirations. Determine the specific skills and knowledge required to succeed in your chosen profession. This could include technical skills, soft skills, industry-specific knowledge, or certifications.

⇨ Create a Development Plan: Once you've identified the skills you need to work on, create a development plan outlining how you will improve them. Break down each skill into smaller, achievable tasks and set deadlines for completing them.

⇨ Seek Learning Opportunities: Take advantage of various learning opportunities to enhance your skills. This could involve enrolling in courses, attending workshops or seminars, reading books or articles, watching tutorials, or seeking mentorship from experts in your field.

⇨ Practice Consistently: Practice is key to mastering any skill. Dedicate time each day or week to practice and refine your skills. Set aside dedicated practice sessions where you can focus solely on improving specific areas.

⇨ Receive Feedback: Seek feedback from others, such as mentors, peers, or supervisors, to gain insights into your progress and areas for improvement. Be open to constructive criticism and use it to refine your skills further.

⇨ Stay Updated: Stay abreast of industry trends, advancements, and changes in your field. Continuously update your skills and knowledge to remain competitive and relevant in the ever-evolving professional landscape.

By following these steps and committing to ongoing skill development, you can enhance your capabilities, boost your confidence, and position yourself for success in your chosen profession. Remember, improvement is a journey, and consistent effort and dedication will lead to continuous growth and advancement.

Mastering these skills—effective communication, negotiation, adaptability, and resilience—not only enhances women's professional capabilities but also empowers them to navigate challenges, seize opportunities, and lead with confidence in their careers. By continuously honing these skills and applying them strategically, women can expand their influence, foster meaningful connections, and make significant contributions to their organizations and communities. Embrace these skills as pillars of your professional toolkit, and pave the way for success and empowerment in your journey ahead.

08

NAVIGATING WORK-LIFE BALANCE

Achieving work-life balance can indeed feel like a roller coaster ride, especially for women juggling multiple responsibilities. However, while it may be challenging, it is certainly not impossible to manage.

Delegating tasks is a powerful strategy for balancing work and life commitments. By identifying tasks that can be delegated to others, whether it's colleagues, family members, or hired help, individuals can free up time and energy to focus on their main priorities. Delegation not only lightens the workload but also fosters collaboration and empowers others to contribute to shared responsibilities.

Prioritization is another key aspect of managing work-life balance. By identifying and focusing on the most important tasks and commitments, individuals can ensure that their time and resources are allocated effectively. This involves setting clear goals, establishing boundaries, and making intentional choices about how to allocate time and energy.

It's important to recognize that achieving work-life balance requires a willingness to make adjustments and prioritize self-care. This may involve saying no to non-essential tasks, setting boundaries around work hours, and making time for activities that nourish the mind, body, and soul.

Ultimately, work-life balance is a personal journey, and there is no one-size-fits-all solution. It requires self-awareness, flexibility, and a commitment to finding harmony between professional and personal responsibilities. By being proactive, resourceful, and resilient, individuals can navigate the ups and downs of work-life balance and create a fulfilling and sustainable lifestyle.

Here's a structured approach to understanding and achieving work-life balance:

- ⇨ Define Your Priorities: Begin by clarifying what matters most to you in both your professional and personal life. Identify your core values, such as family, health, career advancement, or personal growth. Understanding your priorities forms the foundation for making balanced decisions.

- ⇨ Set Boundaries: Establish clear boundaries between work and personal life. This might involve defining specific work hours, unplugging from digital devices during personal time, or setting aside dedicated periods for family and leisure activities. Boundaries help create structure and prevent burnout.

- ⇨ 3. Manage Time Effectively: Prioritize tasks based on importance and deadlines. Use time management techniques such as to-do lists, prioritization frameworks (e.g., Eisenhower Matrix), and scheduling tools to allocate time efficiently between work and personal commitments. Remember to include self-care activities in your schedule.

⇨ Communicate Openly: Foster open communication with your employer, colleagues, and loved ones about your work-life balance needs and expectations. Discuss flexible work arrangements, remote work options, or realistic timelines for projects to accommodate personal responsibilities without compromising professional commitments.

⇨ Delegate and Collaborate:Recognize when to delegate tasks at work and enlist support from family or friends in personal matters. Delegation and collaboration not only lighten your workload but also empower others while fostering a sense of teamwork and shared responsibility.

⇨ Practice Self-Care: Make self-care a priority by engaging in activities that promote physical, mental, and emotional well-being. This includes regular exercise, adequate sleep, mindfulness practices, hobbies, and spending quality time with loved ones. Self-care replenishes your energy and enhances productivity.

⇨ Learn to Say No: Be selective about commitments and learn to say no to requests or tasks that do not align with your priorities or overload your schedule. Setting boundaries and managing workload effectively prevent stress and maintain balance.

⇨ Evaluate and Adjust Regularly: Regularly assess your work-life balance to identify areas that require adjustment. Reflect on what works well and what needs improvement. Adjust your strategies as necessary to align with changing circumstances and evolving priorities.

Achieving work-life balance is an ongoing journey that requires conscious effort, adaptability, and self-awareness. By prioritizing what matters most, setting boundaries, managing time effectively, and practicing self-care, you can navigate work-life balance successfully and lead a fulfilling life that integrates professional achievement with personal well-being.

09

OVERCOMING BARRIERS: DEALING WITH DISCRIMINATION AND BIAS

It's true that women often face various barriers personally, within their families, and within society that can create feelings of fear and hesitation. However, it's essential for women to recognize their own agency and take proactive steps to overcome these barriers.

Taking small, daring steps is a powerful way for women to break free from limitations and open new doors in their lives. This could involve speaking up for oneself, setting boundaries, pursuing education or career opportunities, or advocating for change within their communities.

By stepping outside of their comfort zones and taking risks, women can expand their horizons, discover their strengths, and unlock their full potential. Each daring step taken is a step toward empowerment, independence, and success.

It's important for women to remember that they are capable of overcoming any obstacle or barrier that stands in their way. With courage, determination, and support from others, they can chart their own path and create the life they envision.

Ultimately, by embracing fear and taking daring steps forward, women can inspire others, challenge societal norms, and contribute to positive change in their own lives and the world around them.

Women often face significant challenges in work environments where discrimination and bias are present. Some of the key challenges include:

- ⇨ Pay Inequality: Women frequently encounter disparities in pay compared to their male counterparts, often earning less for the same work or at similar levels of experience and qualification.

- ⇨ Glass Ceiling: Women may find it difficult to advance to higher positions within organizations due to invisible barriers, often limiting their career growth despite their qualifications and achievements.

- ⇨ Gender Stereotypes: Persistent stereotypes can lead to women being pigeonholed into certain roles or assumed to have certain traits (e.g., nurturing rather than leadership qualities), which can hinder their opportunities for career advancement.

- ⇨ Microaggressions: Subtle forms of discrimination, such as dismissive comments, assumptions about capabilities based on gender, or exclusion from informal networks, can create a hostile work environment for women.

⇨ Lack of Representation: In male-dominated industries or leadership positions, the absence of female role models and mentors can make it challenging for women to envision themselves succeeding or accessing support networks.

⇨ Work-Life Balance: Balancing work responsibilities with caregiving and family obligations disproportionately falls on women, impacting their career trajectories and opportunities for advancement.

⇨ Sexual Harassment: Women may face unwanted advances, comments, or behavior of a sexual nature, which not only creates a hostile work environment but can also have lasting psychological and professional repercussions.

⇨ Stereotype Threat: The fear of conforming to negative stereotypes about women's abilities can create additional stress and affect performance in competitive or male-dominated environments.

⇨ Double Standards: Women often face scrutiny and judgment based on their appearance, demeanor, or personal life choices in ways that their male colleagues do not, impacting perceptions of professionalism and credibility.

⇨ Isolation and Belonging: Feeling isolated or not fully included in workplace culture and decision-making processes can lead to feelings of alienation and reduced job satisfaction among women.

Navigating these challenges requires proactive efforts from organizations to address systemic biases, promote inclusive policies, provide mentorship and support networks, and cultivate a culture of respect and equity.

CELEBRATING SUCCESS: STORIES OF EMPOWERMENT

Once we break free from barriers and limited thinking, the possibilities become endless, and we can achieve anything we set our minds to. The mere thought of becoming financially independent fills us with confidence and excitement, and envisioning that future success fuels our motivation to pursue our goals relentlessly.

Stepping out of our comfort zones and seizing opportunities not only boosts our confidence but also opens doors to new experiences, growth, and fulfillment. It's a journey of self-discovery and empowerment, where every achievement, no matter how small, brings us closer to our dreams.

Imagining the happiness and satisfaction that come with achieving our goals is a powerful motivator that propels us forward on our journey. And with determination, perseverance, and a positive mindset, we can turn those dreams into reality and experience the joy of success firsthand.

So, to all those who dare to dream and strive for greatness, remember that the power to create the life you desire lies within you. Break free from limitations, embrace opportunities, and enjoy every moment of the journey toward your goals. Success awaits those who are brave enough to pursue it!

Highlighting stories of successful women who have overcome challenges and achieved remarkable success can be incredibly inspiring. Here are a few examples of such women and their achievements:

Unbounded Dreams: Sudha Murthy's Journey of Service and Inspiration

Sudha Murthy's journey is indeed remarkable and serves as an inspiration to many. Here's a deeper look into her story and contributions:

Sudha Murthy, born in a middle-class family in Shiggaon, Karnataka, grew up with a strong belief in education and self-reliance. Despite societal norms at the time that limited career opportunities for women, she pursued her education with determination. Sudha earned her engineering degree from B.V.B. College of Engineering and Technology in Hubli, and later went on to complete her M.Tech from the Indian Institute of Science in Bangalore.

After completing her education, Sudha Murthy worked briefly as a development engineer at TELCO (now Tata Motors) in Pune. However, her life took a significant turn when she met and married N.R. Narayana Murthy, who would later co-found Infosys.

While Sudha Murthy is often recognized as the supportive wife of Narayana Murthy, her own accomplishments and contributions to society are equally profound. She played a crucial role in the early days of Infosys by handling the administrative and operational aspects of the company while Narayana Murthy focused on the technical and strategic aspects. Her involvement was instrumental in shaping Infosys into one of India's leading I.T. companies.

Beyond her role in Infosys, Sudha Murthy is renowned for her philanthropic work through the Infosys Foundation, which she founded in 1996. Under her leadership, the foundation has supported numerous social welfare and development initiatives in areas such as education, healthcare, rural development, and women's empowerment. The foundation's projects have positively impacted countless lives across India.

Sudha Murthy is also a prolific writer in both English and Kannada, with several novels, short stories, and children's books to her credit. Her writing often reflects her deep empathy for societal issues and her commitment to bringing about positive change.

Her journey from a middle-class upbringing to becoming a pillar of support and leadership in building Infosys, coupled with her philanthropic efforts and literary contributions, exemplifies courage, resilience, and a steadfast commitment to making a difference. Sudha Murthy continues to inspire many with her humility, dedication, and unwavering belief in the power of education and compassion.

❖ *A woman should not be judged by her family background, education, economic status, beauty, or social status. Instead, she should be judged by her thoughts, actions, and beliefs*

❖ *Education and empowerment are the only tools that can bring a change in society. Educate a woman, and you educate a generation*

❖ *Empowerment of women leads to the empowerment of the community and society as a whole*

❖ *Women should never wait for someone to bring change in their lives. They must be the change they want to see*

❖ *Every woman should have the confidence to stand up for herself and the courage to follow her dreams*

❖ *Don't limit yourself because you are a woman; dream big, aim high, and achieve greatness*

❖ *Equality is not a concept. It's not something we should be striving for. It's a necessity. Equality is like gravity. We need it to stand on this earth as men and women*

❖ *The strength of a woman is not measured by the impact that all her hardships in life have had on her, but by the extent of her refusal to allow those hardships to dictate her and who she becomes*

❖ *Real empowerment comes from going beyond yourself and helping others*

❖ *The most effective way to do it is to do it. Stop waiting for things to happen, go out and make them happen*

From Darkness to Light: The Inspiring Journey of Kalpana Saroj

Kalpana Saroj is a notable Indian entrepreneur and social activist whose life story is both inspiring and influential. Here are the key aspects of Kalpana Saroj's life:

Kalpana Saroj was born into a Dalit family in Roperkheda village, Maharashtra, India.

Her childhood was marked by poverty and social challenges, including early marriage at the age of 12, which led to significant personal hardships.

Despite facing early setbacks, including an abusive marriage, Kalpana Saroj displayed remarkable resilience and determination to change her circumstances.

She eventually left her marriage and returned to her parent's home, determined to build a better future for herself.

Kalpana Saroj began her entrepreneurial journey by taking up odd jobs and saving money to start her own tailoring business.

She later expanded into real estate and construction, founding Kamani Tubes, a successful steel pipe manufacturing company, which she acquired when it was on the verge of bankruptcy.

In 2006, Kalpana Saroj acquired Kamani Tubes through a bidding process despite stiff competition. The company was heavily in debt and facing bankruptcy.

Through her leadership and strategic decisions, she successfully turned Kamani Tubes into a profitable enterprise, saving hundreds of jobs in the process.

Beyond her entrepreneurial success, Kalpana Saroj is known for her commitment to social causes, particularly advocating for the rights and empowerment of women and marginalized communities.

She has been actively involved in initiatives aimed at supporting entrepreneurship among women and Dalits, promoting education, and empowering disadvantaged youth.

Kalpana Saroj's achievements have earned her numerous accolades and recognition, including being featured in Forbes Asia's list of 50 Power Businesswomen in Asia-Pacific.

She is a role model for aspiring entrepreneurs, especially women and individuals from marginalized communities, demonstrating that with determination and hard work, one can overcome adversity and achieve success.

Kalpana Saroj's life story exemplifies resilience, courage, and the power of determination in the face of adversity.

She continues to inspire others through her actions, advocating for social justice and economic empowerment and using her platform to uplift and support marginalized communities.

Kalpana Saroj's journey from poverty and hardship to becoming a successful entrepreneur and advocate for social change serves as a powerful example of how individuals can overcome challenges and make a significant impact in their communities and beyond. Her story inspires many to pursue their dreams and contribute positively to society despite obstacles along the way.

Here are some notable Indian women who transitioned from being housewives to becoming influential leaders in various fields:

Kalpana Saroj is known for her inspiring journey from poverty and adversity to becoming a successful entrepreneur and philanthropist. Here are some powerful quotes attributed to her:

- ❖ *If you have courage, determination, and belief in yourself, no obstacle in the world can stop you from achieving your goals.*

- ❖ *Success doesn't come to those who wait for it. It comes to those who work for it*

- ❖ *Difficulties in life are not obstacles; they are stepping stones to success*

- ❖ *Don't be afraid of failures; they are the stepping stones to success*

- ❖ *Believe in yourself and the world will be at your feet*

These quotes reflect Kalpana Saroj's resilience, determination, and belief in the power of hard work and perseverance, inspiring others to overcome challenges and achieve their dreams.

Voices of the Marginalized: The Courageous Journey of Medha Patkar

Medha Patkar is a prominent social activist in India known for her relentless advocacy for the rights of marginalized communities, particularly those affected by large-scale development projects. Here's a narrative of her journey:

Born in Mumbai, India, Medha Patkar grew up with a deep awareness of social inequality and injustice. Her upbringing instilled in her a strong sense of empathy and a desire to bring about positive change in society. After completing her education in social work, she began her journey as an activist in the late 1970s, focusing initially on issues of slum dwellers' rights and urban poverty.

Medha Patkar's activism gained national attention when she co-founded the Narmada Bachao Andolan (NBA) in the early 1980s. The NBA became a significant grassroots movement protesting against large dams on the Narmada River, which were displacing thousands of people and disrupting their livelihoods. Medha Patkar emerged as a prominent voice against the displacement of communities without adequate rehabilitation and the environmental impact of such projects.

Her leadership and unwavering commitment to the cause led to intense advocacy campaigns, protests, and legal battles. Medha Patkar and the NBA successfully raised awareness about the rights of displaced people and influenced policy discussions on sustainable development and social justice in India. Despite facing challenges, including arrests and physical assaults, she continued to mobilize support and draw international attention to the plight of those affected by large-scale infrastructure projects.

Beyond the Narmada Bachao Andolan, Medha Patkar has been involved in various social movements advocating for the rights of farmers, laborers, and marginalized communities across India. She has spoken out against corruption, inequality, and exploitation, championing causes that often go unnoticed or are marginalized in mainstream discourse.

Medha Patkar's legacy is one of courage, resilience, and unwavering dedication to social justice. Her journey is a testament to the power of grassroots activism and the importance of standing up for the rights of the disenfranchised. Through her actions and advocacy, she continues to inspire countless individuals and organizations to strive for a more just and equitable society.

Medha Patkar's story exemplifies how one person's determination and commitment can catalyze movements for social change and justice, leaving a lasting impact on communities and society at large.

Some powerful quotes attributed to Medha Patkar:

- ❖ *The struggle of the people is my struggle; their aspirations are my aspirations*
- ❖ *Development that ignores human rights, social justice, and environmental sustainability is not development at all*

❖ *We cannot accept development that displaces millions and benefits only a few*

❖ *Justice delayed is justice denied, and we cannot wait for justice indefinitely*

❖ *Activism is the rent I pay for living on this planet*

These quotes reflect Medha Patkar's steadfast commitment to social justice, human rights, and environmental sustainability through her activism and advocacy work. She has consistently spoken out against injustice and fought for the rights of marginalized communities in India, making a significant impact on social movements and policy discussions.

Mary Kom: A Fighter's Journey

Mary Kom, born Mangte Chungneijang Mary Kom, hails from a humble background in Manipur, India. From a young age, she displayed a natural talent and passion for boxing, a sport typically dominated by men in India. Despite societal norms and financial constraints, Mary Kom pursued her dream relentlessly.

Her journey to greatness was fraught with challenges. She faced opposition from her community and struggled to find adequate training facilities and support. Undeterred, Mary Kom trained rigorously, often juggling her boxing career with family responsibilities. Her determination and resilience saw her rise through the ranks, becoming a national champion and earning the nickname "Magnificent Mary."

Mary Kom's breakthrough came in 2002 when she won her first gold medal at the Women's World Boxing Championships in Turkey, marking the beginning of her illustrious international career. Over the years, she continued to defy odds and clinch medals at various prestigious tournaments, including multiple golds at the Asian Games and Commonwealth Games.

Beyond her sporting achievements, Mary Kom is celebrated for breaking barriers and inspiring generations of women. She has become an icon of empowerment, demonstrating that with grit and perseverance, anything is possible. Her story is a testament to the power of determination, passion, and belief in oneself, transcending boundaries and inspiring millions around the world.

Today, Mary Kom continues to train rigorously and mentor aspiring boxers. She remains a beacon of hope and inspiration, proving that no obstacle is insurmountable for those who dare to dream and work tirelessly to achieve their goals. Her journey embodies the spirit of resilience and determination, making her a true inspiration and role model for individuals everywhere.

Mary Kom, the legendary Indian boxer, has inspired many with her words of wisdom and determination. Here are some powerful quotes attributed to her:

* ❖ *Don't let anyone tell you you're weak because you're a woman*

> ❖ *I don't care about what people think of me, I'm out there to prove myself*
>
> ❖ *If you have confidence in your ability and strength, you can do anything*
>
> ❖ *Hard work and dedication is the only way to succeed*
>
> ❖ *I have competed in every corner of the world, I've fought and won against the best boxers on the planet. This is my life's dream and I'm not going to let anyone stop me*
>
> *These quotes reflect Mary Kom's resilience, determination, and belief in herself, inspiring countless individuals to pursue their dreams with courage and conviction*

Beyond Borders: The Priyanka Chopra Jonas Journey

Priyanka Chopra Jonas, born in Jamshedpur, India, began her journey to stardom with aspirations to make a mark in the entertainment industry. Her childhood was marked by academic excellence and a passion for performing arts. Priyanka's entry into the world of beauty pageants in the early 2000s catapulted her into the limelight, winning the Miss World title in 2000.

Priyanka's debut in Bollywood came shortly after, marking the beginning of a successful acting career. She quickly gained recognition for her versatility and ability to portray diverse characters with depth and authenticity. Her breakout role in "Fashion" (2008) earned her critical acclaim and several awards, solidifying her position as a leading actress in Indian cinema.

Beyond Bollywood, Priyanka's ambition and determination propelled her toward international recognition. In 2015, she made her debut on American television with the series "Quantico," where she played the role of Alex Parrish—a character who showcased her acting prowess and charisma to a global audience. The show's success not only cemented Priyanka's status as a cross-over star but also opened doors to Hollywood.

Priyanka Chopra Jonas's journey is not merely about acting accolades but also about breaking barriers and reshaping perceptions. As a woman of South Asian descent, she has been a vocal advocate for diversity and representation in entertainment. Her roles in films like "Baywatch" (2017) and "The Sky Is Pink" (2019) further demonstrated her range as an actress and her commitment to storytelling that resonates with audiences worldwide.

Priyanka's influence extends beyond the silver screen. She is a UNICEF Goodwill Ambassador, actively advocating for children's rights and gender equality. Her philanthropic work includes supporting educational initiatives and empowering marginalized communities, reflecting her dedication to making a positive impact beyond the entertainment industry.

Today, Priyanka Chopra Jonas continues to inspire millions with her journey from a small-town girl with big dreams to a global icon. Her resilience, determination, and unwavering belief in herself serve as a beacon of empowerment for individuals striving to defy the odds and achieve their aspirations, regardless of their background or circumstances.

Some powerful quotes attributed to Priyanka Chopra Jonas:

❖ *My dad always said, 'You should not fit into any stereotype. You should always make your own path*

❖ *I believe destiny and hard work go hand in hand. I was studying to be an engineer when my mom and my brother sent my pictures for the Miss India contest. I didn't even know about it. If that isn't destiny, what is*

❖ *I think it's great to be flawed. I am hugely flawed, and I like it this way. That's the fun of life. You fall, get up, make mistakes, learn from them, be human and be you."*

❖ *I was raised to be fearless when it came to opinions. I was always encouraged to have an opinion, have a voice."*

❖ *5You can't be afraid of failure. It's the only way you succeed—you're not gonna succeed all the time, and I know that."*

These quotes reflect Priyanka Chopra Jonas's perspective on life, resilience, self-confidence, and the importance of embracing one's flaws and failures as part of the journey to success.

Kiran Bedi: A Trailblazer in Indian Law Enforcement

Kiran Bedi, born on June 9, 1949, in Amritsar, Punjab, India, emerged as a pioneer in the Indian Police Service (IPS) and later in the realm of social activism and governance.

Her journey is marked by numerous achievements and a relentless commitment to reform and public service.

From a young age, Kiran Bedi displayed academic excellence and a passion for sports. She excelled in tennis and academics, earning a Bachelor of Arts degree in English from Government College for Women, Amritsar, and later a Master's degree in Political Science from Punjab University, Chandigarh. Her interest in social justice and public service led her to join the Indian Police Service in 1972, becoming the first woman to do so.

During her tenure in the IPS, Kiran Bedi gained recognition for her tough stance on crime and corruption. She introduced several innovative measures to improve prison conditions and rehabilitation programs, earning her the nickname "Crane Bedi" for towing illegally parked vehicles and "Iron Lady" for her strong-willed approach to law enforcement.

One of her most significant contributions was transforming the Tihar Jail, one of the largest prisons in India, into a model institution known for its focus on education, vocational training, and rehabilitation. Her initiatives significantly reduced violence and recidivism rates among inmates, garnering international acclaim and recognition.

Beyond her career in law enforcement, Kiran Bedi has been a vocal advocate for social causes, including women's empowerment, education, and healthcare. She founded several NGOs and initiatives aimed at promoting literacy, health awareness, and community development, impacting the lives of thousands across India.

Kiran Bedi's journey is a testament to courage, leadership, and dedication to public service. Her pioneering spirit has inspired generations of women to break barriers and pursue careers in law enforcement and social activism. Today, she continues to be an influential voice in India, advocating for transparency, accountability, and the empowerment of marginalized communities. Her legacy remains a shining example of the transformative power of leadership and compassion in service to society.

Certainly! Kiran Bedi is known for her strong convictions and commitment to public service. Here are Some powerful quotes attributed to heri:

1. "Don't limit your challenges. Challenge your limits."

2. "If you dare, nothing can stop you."

3. "Do your duty with integrity. Give without expectations. Love without conditions. Live without regrets."

4. "Be the change you wish to see in the world."

5. "It's not enough to be good. We must strive to be great."

These quotes reflect Kiran Bedi's philosophy on leadership, courage, integrity, and the importance of striving for excellence in every endeavor. She has been a trailblazer in law enforcement and social activism in India, inspiring many with her actions and words.

Oprah Winfrey: The Journey of a Media Mogul and Philanthropist

Oprah Winfrey, born on January 29, 1954, in Kosciusko, Mississippi, USA, rose from challenging beginnings to become one of the most influential figures in media and philanthropy. Her story is one of resilience, determination, and a commitment to empowering others through her work.

Growing up in poverty and facing significant challenges, including abuse and hardship, Oprah found solace in education and public speaking. She began her career in media at a young age, working as a news anchor and reporter. In 1984, she launched "The Oprah Winfrey Show," which quickly became one of the highest-rated television programs in history.

Oprah's unique ability to connect with her audience, empathize with their struggles, and openly share her own experiences contributed to the show's immense popularity. She tackled a wide range of topics, from personal development and relationships to social issues and current events, always advocating for positivity, self-improvement, and empowerment.

Beyond her television career, Oprah Winfrey ventured into film production, founding Harpo Productions and later launching the OWN (Oprah Winfrey Network) television channel. She used her platform to amplify diverse voices, promote storytelling that inspires and uplifts, and address important social issues such as education, healthcare, and women's rights.

Oprah's impact extends far beyond the entertainment industry. She is a passionate philanthropist, supporting causes related to education, child welfare, and empowerment through her Oprah Winfrey Foundation and various charitable initiatives. Her contributions to society have earned her numerous accolades, including the Presidential Medal of Freedom in 2013.

Throughout her career, Oprah Winfrey has demonstrated resilience in the face of adversity, a commitment to continuous self-improvement, and a belief in the power of storytelling to effect positive change. Her journey from a difficult childhood to becoming a global media icon and philanthropist serves as an inspiration to millions worldwide, proving that with determination, authenticity, and compassion, one can overcome any obstacle and make a lasting impact on society.

> *Certainly! Oprah Winfrey is known for her insightful and empowering quotes that resonate with people around the world. Here are some powerful quotes attributed to her:*
>
> ❖ *Turn your wounds into wisdom*
>
> ❖ *The biggest adventure you can take is to live the life of your dreams*
>
> ❖ *Think like a queen. A queen is not afraid to fail. Failure is another steppingstone to greatness*

> ❖ *Surround yourself with only people who are going to lift you higher*
>
> ❖ *The more you praise and celebrate your life, the more there is in life to celebrate*
>
> *These quotes reflect Oprah Winfrey's wisdom, positivity, and belief in personal growth and empowerment. She has inspired countless individuals to pursue their dreams, embrace their authenticity, and strive for greatness in all aspects of life.*

I Am Malala: The Courageous Journey for Education and Equality

Malala Yousafzai, born on July 12, 1997, in Mingora, Pakistan, emerged as a global symbol of courage, resilience, and advocacy for girls' education. Her journey is marked by bravery in the face of adversity and a steadfast commitment to promoting education and equality.

Growing up in the Swat Valley region of Pakistan, Malala's father, Ziauddin Yousafzai, was an advocate for education and encouraged Malala and her peers to pursue learning despite the challenges posed by the Taliban's increasing influence. Malala herself became an outspoken advocate for girls' education, blogging anonymously for BBC Urdu under the pseudonym Gul Makai, detailing life under Taliban rule and the struggle for education.

In October 2012, tragedy struck when Malala was shot in the head by Taliban gunmen while riding a bus home from school. The assassination attempt, intended to silence her activism, instead amplified her voice on the global stage. Malala survived the attack and underwent extensive medical treatment in the United Kingdom, where she and her family eventually settled.

Following her recovery, Malala continued her advocacy work with even greater determination. She co-authored the memoir "I Am Malala," which became an international bestseller and further raised awareness about the importance of education and the plight of girls in regions affected by conflict and extremism.

Malala's activism garnered widespread recognition, culminating in her being awarded the Nobel Peace Prize in 2014, becoming the youngest-ever Nobel laureate at the age of 17. The prize recognized her courageous advocacy for girls' education and her continued efforts to empower young women worldwide through the Malala Fund, an organization she co-founded with her father to champion education for girls globally.

Today, Malala Yousafzai continues to be a leading voice for girls' rights and education. She has become an inspiration to millions, demonstrating the transformative power of education and the resilience of the human spirit in overcoming adversity. Her story serves as a reminder of the importance of standing up for what is right and the impact that one individual can have on shaping a more just and equitable world.

Malala Yousafzai is known for her powerful and inspiring words that have resonated with people around the world. Here are some quotes attributed to Malala Yousafzai:

- *We realize the importance of our voices only when we are silenced*

- *Let us pick up our books and our pens, they are the most powerful weapons*

- *One child, one teacher, one book, one pen can change the world*

- *I raise up my voice—not so I can shout, but so that those without a voice can be heard*

- *When the whole world is silent, even one voice becomes powerful*

These quotes reflect Malala Yousafzai's courage, advocacy for education and equality, and her belief in the power of individuals to make a difference in the world. Her words continue to inspire and empower people of all ages to stand up for their rights and work toward positive change in their communities and beyond.

Arundhati Roy: The Writer and Activist Who Redefines Courage

Arundhati Roy, born on November 24, 1961, in Shillong, India, is renowned for her powerful storytelling and fearless advocacy for social justice and human rights. Her journey from a childhood marked by wanderlust and a love for books to becoming a globally acclaimed author and activist is as compelling as her literary works.

Roy's literary career was launched spectacularly with her debut novel, "The God of Small Things," published in 1997. The novel, set in Kerala, India, intricately weaves together themes of love, caste, family, and societal norms, winning the prestigious Booker Prize and catapulting Roy to international acclaim. Her lyrical prose and bold narrative style captured the hearts of readers worldwide, establishing her as a formidable literary voice.

However, Arundhati Roy's impact extends beyond the realm of literature. She has consistently used her platform and influence to speak out against injustices, environmental degradation, and the marginalization of oppressed communities. Her outspoken activism has often courted controversy but has also sparked crucial conversations on issues ranging from government policies to corporate greed and social inequality.

Roy's commitment to social justice is evident in her essays, speeches, and non-fiction works, where she fearlessly challenges power structures and advocates for marginalized voices. She has been a vocal critic of globalization, neoliberalism, and the erosion of democratic values, urging individuals and governments to prioritize human rights and environmental sustainability.

In addition to her writing and activism, Arundhati Roy has been involved in grassroots movements and campaigns, actively supporting causes such as environmental conservation, indigenous rights, and gender equality. She continues to engage in public discourse, delivering lectures and participating in debates that shape public opinion and policy discourse in India and globally.

Arundhati Roy's story is a testament to the power of words and activism in effecting social change. Through her courage, intellect, and unwavering commitment to justice, she inspires countless individuals to question the status quo and strive for a more equitable and compassionate world.

Arundhati Roy is known for her eloquent and thought-provoking quotes that challenge conventional wisdom and provoke introspection. Here are some inspiring quotes attributed to her:

❖ *Another world is not only possible, she is on her way. On a quiet day, I can hear her breathing."*

❖ *To love. To be loved. To never forget your own insignificance. To never get used to the unspeakable violence and the vulgar disparity of life around you. To seek joy in the saddest places. To pursue beauty to its lair. To never simplify what is complicated or complicate what is simple. To respect strength, never power. Above all, to watch. To try and understand. To never look away. And never, never to forget."*

❖ *The only dream worth having is to dream that you will live while you're alive and die only when you're dead. To love. To be loved. To never forget your own insignificance. To never get used to the unspeakable violence and the vulgar disparity of life around you. To seek joy in the saddest places. To pursue beauty to its lair. To never simplify what is complicated or complicate what is simple. To respect strength, never power. Above all, to watch. To try and understand. To never look away. And never, never to forget."*

Kalpana Chawla: Reaching for the Stars

Kalpana Chawla, born on March 17, 1962, in Karnal, Haryana, India, was a trailblazing astronaut and the first woman of Indian origin in space. Her inspiring journey from a small town in India to the stars is a testament to perseverance, dedication, and the pursuit of dreams.

Kalpana's passion for flying began at a young age. Despite facing challenges and societal expectations, she pursued her dreams with unwavering determination. After earning a degree in Aeronautical Engineering from Punjab Engineering College, she moved to the United States to further her education and obtained a Master's degree in Aerospace Engineering and a PhD in Aerospace Engineering from the University of Colorado Boulder.

In 1994, Kalpana was selected by NASA for their astronaut program, where she underwent rigorous training and preparation. Her first space mission came in 1997 aboard the Space Shuttle Columbia as a mission specialist and primary robotic arm operator. This historic flight made her the first woman of Indian descent to travel to space, achieving a lifelong dream and inspiring millions around the world.

Kalpana's contributions to space exploration were significant. During her missions, she conducted experiments related to microgravity and materials science, advancing our understanding of space technology and its applications. Her dedication and professionalism earned her admiration and respect from colleagues and space enthusiasts alike.

Tragically, Kalpana Chawla lost her life in the Space Shuttle Columbia disaster on February 1, 2003, when the shuttle disintegrated upon re-entry into earth's atmosphere. Her courage and pioneering spirit continue to inspire generations, and she remains a symbol of perseverance and the limitless possibilities of human achievement.

Kalpana Chawla's legacy lives on through her contributions to science, her determination to defy boundaries, and her enduring impact on space exploration. Her story serves as a beacon of hope and inspiration, encouraging others to reach for the stars and pursue their dreams, no matter how challenging the journey may be.

Learning from the stories of successful women who have managed to balance marriage and family responsibilities and pursue their dreams can be incredibly inspiring and empowering. Each of these women has navigated challenges and overcome obstacles to achieve remarkable success in their respective fields. Here's a motivational message that encapsulates their journeys:

Fly with Your Wings: Embracing Success After Marriage

In a world where societal expectations often place limits on what women can achieve after marriage, the stories of extraordinary women like Sudha Murthy, Priyanka Chopra, Mary Kom, Kalpana Chawla, Arundhati Roy, Oprah Winfrey, Kiran Bedi, Medha Patkar, and Kalpana Saroj stand as powerful examples of breaking barriers and pursuing dreams with unwavering determination.

Sudha Murthy, through her philanthropy and leadership, has shown how one can balance family commitments while making significant contributions to society. **Priyanka Chopra**, a global icon, has exemplified resilience and ambition by excelling in acting, entrepreneurship, and humanitarian work despite global fame and personal commitments. **Mary Kom**, the boxing champion, has proven that with dedication and hard work, one can achieve greatness in sports while managing a family.

Kalpana Chawla, the astronaut, soared to the stars, demonstrating that even the sky is not the limit when one is driven by passion and purpose. **Arundhati Roy**, through her writing and activism, has challenged societal norms and advocated for justice, inspiring countless individuals worldwide. **Malala Yousafzai**, despite adversity, continues to champion education and women's rights globally, showing that courage knows no bounds.

Oprah Winfrey, from a troubled childhood to becoming a media mogul and philanthropist, exemplifies resilience and the power of self-belief in achieving one's dreams. **Kiran Bedi**, India's first female IPS officer, broke gender stereotypes in law enforcement, paving the way for women in leadership roles. **Medha Patkar**, the social activist, has dedicated her life to advocating for marginalized communities, showcasing the impact of passion and dedication in creating societal change.

Kalpana Saroj, from adversity to entrepreneurship, has shown that with determination and resilience, one can overcome challenges and build a successful business empire.

These remarkable women have shown us that marriage and family life need not be barriers to personal and professional fulfillment. They have demonstrated that with courage, perseverance, and a supportive environment, women can achieve their aspirations and make a difference in the world. Their stories remind us that it is never too late to pursue our dreams, spread our wings, and soar toward our goals.

So, to all the women out there: Don't let anyone or anything stop you from pursuing your dreams. Embrace your aspirations, manage your challenges with grace, and believe in the power of your dreams. Fly with your wings, reach for your goals, and let your journey inspire others to do the same.

Conclusion:

Embracing Empowerment

As we come to the culmination of this journey through the lives and stories of empowered homemakers, it is evident that the narrative of balancing personal and professional aspirations is not just about managing tasks but about embracing empowerment in its fullest sense. Throughout this book, we have explored the challenges, triumphs, and inspiring journeys of women who have redefined the traditional roles of homemakers, breaking boundaries and forging paths that integrate both familial responsibilities and personal ambitions.

Reflecting on Resilience

At the heart of every story shared in these pages lies a narrative of resilience. We have witnessed women who have faced adversity with unwavering determination, whether it was balancing the demands of a burgeoning career with the joys of motherhood or navigating societal expectations while pursuing personal passions. Their resilience teaches us that setbacks are not roadblocks but opportunities for growth and transformation.

Empowerment through Choice

Central to the theme of empowerment is the notion of choice. The women we have encountered in these pages have made deliberate choices—sometimes difficult and unconventional—that have enabled them to shape their own destinies. They have challenged norms, embraced their unique strengths, and defied expectations, illustrating that true empowerment begins with recognizing one's agency to choose and act.

Breaking Societal Norms

The journey of empowered homemakers is also a narrative of breaking societal norms and redefining success on their own terms. These women have shattered stereotypes and expanded the boundaries of what it means to be a homemaker. They have proven that homemaking is not synonymous with limitation but can be a platform for creativity, entrepreneurship, and leadership.

Balancing Acts: Navigating Dual Realities

Throughout this exploration, we have delved into the intricacies of balancing dual realities—the personal and the professional. We have discussed practical strategies for time management, effective communication, and self-care that enable women to thrive in both spheres without compromising their well-being. The stories shared have underscored the importance of flexibility, support networks, and the ability to adapt to changing circumstances.

Celebrating Success and Lessons Learned

As we celebrate the successes and lessons learned from the empowered homemakers featured in this book, it is crucial to recognize that their journeys are not just individual achievements but collective triumphs that inspire and pave the way for future generations. Their stories serve as guiding lights for those navigating similar paths, offering insights into resilience, courage, and the pursuit of fulfillment.

Looking Forward: A Call to Action

Looking forward, the journey toward empowerment is ongoing. It requires continuous reflection, adaptation, and advocacy for systemic change that supports women in achieving their full potential. It calls for dismantling barriers, fostering inclusive environments, and amplifying diverse voices that enrich our understanding of what it means to be an empowered homemaker in the 21st century.

A New Narrative of Empowerment

In conclusion, *Empowered Homemakers – Breaking Boundaries* is not just a book but a testament to the power of storytelling and the transformative potential of empowered women. It challenges us to rethink traditional narratives and envision a future where homemakers are valued not only for their caregiving roles but also for their leadership, innovation, and resilience. Let this book serve as a catalyst for conversations, actions, and aspirations that empower homemakers everywhere to break boundaries, embrace their full potential, and contribute meaningfully to society.

These conclusion notes aim to encapsulate the themes explored throughout the book while providing a call to action and inspiration for readers to embrace empowerment in their own lives.